D0821716

HARRIET CHALMERS ADAMS
Explorer and Adventurer

Notable Americans

HARRIET CHALMERS ADAMS
Explorer and Adventurer

Durlynn Anema

MORGAN
REYNOLDS
Incorporated

Greensboro

HARRIET CHALMERS ADAMS *Explorer and Adventurer*

Photo credits: cover, pp. 11, 15, 21, 23, 25, 37, 59, 61, 65, 67, 71, 77, 83, 85, Bank of
Stockton Archives; pp. 47, 53, National Geographic Society; p. 95, Society of Woman
Geographers.

Library of Congress Cataloging-in-Publication Data
Anema, Durlynn.
  Harriet Chalmers Adams : explorer and adventurer / Durlynn Anema.
    p. cm. — (Notable Americans)
  Includes bibliographical references and index.
  Summary: Relates the life of the woman recognized as an explorer, writer, photographer,
lecturer, and citizen of the globe concerned for native people throughout the world.
    ISBN 1-883846-18-8 (hardcover)
    1. Adams, Harriet Chalmers, 1875-1937—Juvenile literature. 2. Explorers—United
States—Biography—Juvenile literature. 3. Women explorers—United States—Biogra-
phy—Juvenile literature. 4. Women adventurers—United States—Biography—Juvenile
literature. 5. Photographers—United States—Biography—Juvenile literature. 6. Women
photographers—United States—Biography—Juvenile literature.   [1. Adams, Harriet
Chalmers, 1875-1937. 2. Explorers. 3. Adventure and adventurers. 4. Photographers. 5.
Women—Biography] I. Title II. Series.
CT275. A28A64 1997
910'.92—dc21

96-54642
CIP

Printed in the United States of America

First Edition

Dedicated to the members of the Harriet Chalmers Adams Society, Stockton, California, whose nomination motivated me to research and write about their "hometown" heroine.

ACKNOWLEDGEMENTS

All books are written with the help of a multitude of people—and this one is no exception. For research aid thanks to Beverly Hine, Reference Librarian, Stockton Public Library and her wonderful staff who allowed me to wander through the California history stacks and peruse Harriet's scrapbooks; Janice Kruger, administrator, Society of Woman Geographers; Rene Braden, archivist, National Geographic Society; Rob Schmelzer, NSG Image Collection, National Geographic Society; Beverly Wheaton-Lake, archivist, Organization of American States; Stella Villagen, librarian, Organization of American States and her staff for allowing me free run of their library materials; Lorrayne Kennedy, archivist, Calaveras County, California; Russell B. Adams, Jr., descendent of Franklin P. Adams' father Henry. Leslie Crowe, archivist, Bank of Stockton, reproduced the photographs in this book from copies found in the scrapbooks.Thanks to Leslie and Bank of Stockton. Special appreciation to Kate Davis whose Thesis on Harriet and her recording of Harriet's Latin American journals made this project much easier.To the members of the Harriet Chalmers Adams Society, Stockton, California—warm appreciation for nominating me and involving me with a special woman in history. Without your organization, this book never would have become reality. Finally -- thanks to Vern Garten, my husband, who put up with hours of researching—and writing—and rewriting. Let's take a trip to South America!

CONTENTS

Riding the Mountain Trails 9

Into the Unknown 18

Vampire Bats and Unmapped Regions 28

The Old Inca Highway 41

Jungle Depths and Island Bliss 50

Telling the South America Tale 56

The Routes of Columbus 63

Native Origins 69

War Correspondent 79

Return to South America 88

Founding A Society 93

Final Journey 98

Bibliography 106

Index 110

RIDING THE MOUNTAIN TRAILS

Harriet Chalmers always remembered the first time her father tossed her into the saddle in front of him and rode toward the mountains. It was two summers after her birth in Stockton, California on October 22, 1875. "My father had no boys, so I took a boy's place. I always rode with him and learned to love the out of doors," Harriet later commented. "Our summers were spent in the saddle." While her mother and younger sister enjoyed vacationing at resorts, Harriet and her father, Alexander Chalmers, explored. Their journeys took them from the Sierra foothills to the mountain peaks, from the central valley of California to the seacoast, and occasionally to the Rocky Mountains of her father's native Canada.

At eight-years-old, Harriet and her father made a horseback trip through the San Joaquin and Sacramento valleys and along the California coast. "That journey made me over, from a domestic little girl . . . to one who wished to go to the ends of the earth and to see and study the people of all lands," Harriet said.

Harriet inherited her passion for travel from her father. He had traveled from Canada to California as a young man. He hoped to get rich mining gold in the American River. In 1868 he gave up mining and opened Chalmers Brothers Dry Goods and Carpets in Stockton with his brother George. Harriet inherited her compulsion to read from her mother, Fannie. Her mother's family had come to California in the 1850s, soon after gold had been discovered at Sutter's Mill.

Stockton, lying in California's San Joaquin Valley east of San Francisco, was a perfect location for journeys in every direction. The San Joaquin River joined the Sacramento River, which together flowed to San Pablo Bay, then on to San Francisco. Boat trips to San Francisco and Sacramento were a regular occurrence.

Harriet loved to sit on the river banks and watch ships pull along the wooden docks. They loaded grain, produce, cattle and ore from surrounding farms, ranches and mines, and unloaded supplies for the city and the mining districts to the east. This was a bustling era for Stockton, and the Chalmers family was an integral part of the activity. Harriet often visited the dry goods store to listen to her father entertain the store's customers with tales of his previous adventures.

When by herself, she sometimes boarded the horse car that was Stockton's main transportation and explored south, east and north (west was the river).

Trips into the foothills occupied many of Harriet and Alexander's weekends. His mining interests often took them to Calaveras County, forty miles east of Stockton. On their

Harriet's childhood was spent in this house in Stockton, California.

horseback rides they saw the white basaltic cliffs on the Stanislaus River, natural rock bridges near Vallecito, and a huge underground cave at Cave City.

Both Harriet and Alexander were fascinated by the Cave City area. There were sparkling creeks, pine forests, and beautiful white and rose quartz rock. Later, in the early 1900s, Alexander returned to manage mines there and in Angel's Creek.

Trips to Yosemite State Park (named a national park in 1890) were another highlight of their horseback rides. The beauty of Half Dome at sunrise, the roaring of Yosemite Falls, the lush green meadows and abundant wildlife transfixed the pair.

Throughout Harriet's career, her earliest California travels enhanced her writing and lecturing. Years later, in Fresno, California, she remarked to an audience, "Do you know the last time I walked in my sleep was when I visited Fresno? I awoke at four o'clock in the morning to find myself in my night dress in the middle of the street."

Reading was a pastime Harriet shared with her younger sister Anna and mother. After reading tales of far-away lands, Harriet would exclaim, "Someday I'm going to visit that land. And then I can write my own adventures."

When Harriet was fourteen-years-old, Alexander decided on a long and dangerous journey—to explore California from the Oregon border to Mexico on horseback. Their exploration would concentrate on the crest of the Sierra Nevada Mountain range. Harriet was thrilled with the prospect; her mother was concerned at the journey's length.

Missing too much school was not a problem, however. Since her eleventh birthday, she and her younger sister were taught at home by tutors. This enabled Alexander to take Harriet on explorations. As she grew older, Harriet developed abilities in data collection. She insisted on being thoroughly systematic in all research. Her father taught her how to retain impressions of places visited and sights seen. In addition, she had an affinity for languages, and eventually learned Spanish, Portuguese, Italian, German, and French. Harriet always found it easy to learn the basics of native languages wherever she traveled.

Harriet and Alexander started their year-long exploration in the early spring of 1889, riding to the Oregon border through the Sacramento Valley. Their trail took them past Mt. Shasta at 14,161 feet. (Mt. Lassen, to the south, would become an active volcano in 1912.) Their goal was to progress through the trail's highest sections during summer, then reach the easier, lower elevations by late fall.

Harriet and Alexander spent almost a year in the saddle— crisscrossing the Sierra Nevadas when the weather permitted and arriving in the Southern Mountains as winter approached.

With Harriet's vivid imagination, she pictured herself an Indian princess crossing the high mountain trails on the way to a special ceremony. Or she was the first explorer to these valleys and would later need to describe her findings. In later years, she used her imagination as she lectured and wrote to paint colorful pictures of sights she had seen. She always compared what she saw with these first California memories. By the time they reached the Mexican border, Harriet had crossed many trails in the Sierra Nevada chain. "I was an explorer when I was too young to realize it," she later wrote. The trip helped Harriet decide on her life work. This "wonderful journey stirred powerfully my imagination and set a thousand gypsy spirits to dancing in my blood."

By her late teenage years, Harriet Chalmers could climb high into the trees, swim across the San Joaquin River, and beat the boys at many of their games. She was fearless in all she attempted.

Although Franklin Adams was seven years older than Harriet, he was fascinated by her physical exploits, and by her intelligence. Her enthusiastic discussions of philosophy, history, languages, and far-away lands was different from those of most girls he knew.

Frank had envied Harriet's free, roaming life since he first moved to Stockton. Their paths first crossed because Harriet's father and Frank's older brother Henry were partners in a mine. Henry had also married Harriet's cousin, Etta.

Frank's father had arrived in Monterey, California, in 1844 as a teenager and later became superintendent of the Stockton Gas and Electric Company. Frank graduated from Stockton High School and studied to become an engineer. When he began courting Harriet, he worked at the Stockton Gas and Electric Company alongside his brother Henry.

Despite her love for the outdoors and the physical life, Harriet was petite and ladylike with luxuriant brunette hair

Harriet's father operated Chalmer's Brothers Dry Goods and Carpets.

and lively brown eyes. In later years she would be described as seeming "more at home in a drawing room than leading the rugged life of an explorer." Her mother knew the two sides of her daughter and wondered which life she would choose—adventuring or gentility. Harriet conceded: "I adore good clothes. I can talk dress for hours . . . fitting a new dress is an adventure which appeals almost as much as a new people or a new river to explore."

Frank's courtship of Harriet was patient. She enjoyed the attentions of this serious man with sparkling green eyes and sandy hair. Often they sat on the grassy river bank watching freighters load grain for foreign ports. Where would the ships sail? China? India? The West Indies?

Finally, Frank's persistence won her over and they were married in Stockton on October 5, 1899. While no honeymoon immediately followed the wedding, they agreed to travel abroad as soon as finances and opportunity made it possible. Their first home was a Stockton rooming house. They chose not to settle into a house—more pressing matters concerned them.

Travel remained uppermost in their minds. Fascinated by the first automobiles, they were early motorists. By automobile, train and horse they traveled throughout California that first year of marriage.

They took an extended honeymoon the next year and sailed for Mexico, where Frank worked on an engineering survey.

Harriet was thrilled by Mexico—not the big cities, but the rural areas, historical landmarks and Indian and Mayan archaeological sites. Her history books had related a different story than she experienced. Mexico was full of culture and history. Why hadn't she been taught more about this ancient culture? Had she been misled about other areas of the world? In an effort to learn as much as possible, she scoured archaeological sites. Discovery of the Mayan, Aztec, and other native cultures was then in its infancy. Much remained buried in jungles or under mounds of dirt. Harriet was enthralled by each new site, unearthed ruin, and Indian tribe. She asked questions to penetrate deeper into the unknown.

Frank found Harriet to be an adaptive, eager traveling companion. She quickly adjusted to any terrain, any mode of travel, and was not adverse to lodging in a native hut or to camping in the wild. At the end of their Mexican sojourn, Harriet begged Frank to find more survey work—anything that could keep them traveling.

This first trip to Mexico set the tone for Harriet and Frank's life together. It also laid the foundation for Frank's career with the Pan American Union. He joined their staff in 1907 and worked there until he retired in 1934.

After returning home they settled into the Imperial Hotel and began thinking of their next journey. Wouldn't it be wonderful to travel throughout all of Latin America? To Central and South America?

INTO THE UNKNOWN

The opportunity to travel in Latin America came in 1904 when Frank accepted a job inspecting Central and South American mines. Although the job did not compensate for all expenses, it paid their passage to Latin America.

Harriet began to eagerly research Latin America. She read fifteen books about the region. As she read she slowly realized the immensity of the undertaking. South America contained a country, Brazil, that was larger than the United States at that time. It would take years to see everything.

Harriet and Frank worked out the itinerary for their trip. First they would honor the mining contracts. Then they would follow "the trail of the conquistadors however it leads us, studying the early civilizations, both of the Spaniards and the Incas and others who were there when the Spaniards came."

Harriet planned to write and lecture about the journey. Frank had learned photography during his studies and taught the skill to Harriet. They wanted to visually document their experiences. They decided on colored slides, black and white photographs, and motion pictures, as the best mediums to compliment Harriet's writing. Because the trip was scheduled to take three years, the necessary camera, film and motion picture equipment made for bulky luggage. Riding and hiking boots, split skirts for riding, long-sleeved shirts to repel insects, and warm coats for the chill nights of the Andes also went into the trunks. Gloves and hats—both to protect from the glare of the sun and for warmth in the mountains—were also needed. Even a few party dresses were carefully placed in the trunks for special occasions.

On January 9, 1904, thirty relatives and friends, including Alexander and Fannie Chalmers, gathered on San Francisco's Pier 38 to bid the young couple farewell.

At first Harriet suffered from seasickness, something she would experience throughout her lifetime. Within a couple of days she recovered and was soon on deck enjoying the views as they passed the lower portions of Baja California and "Cape St. Lucas," then sailed across the Gulf of California to Mazatlan. Gray porpoises jumped in the wake. White sea gulls crisscrossed above them, and fish swam along the ship.

As they sailed the coast of Mexico and Central America, they stopped in as many ports as possible. They were eager to travel inland to meet natives and to view scenery. They enjoyed the sights in Acapulco and Guatemala and on January 26 were in El Salvador. They stayed there two weeks.

In El Salvador Harriet developed a taste for chocolate. The senora of the estate where she and Frank stayed made the chocolate from the cocoa trees on the plantation. For the rest of her life, Harriet ate chocolate at every opportunity.

The Adamses arrived in Panama City during a chaotic time. A revolt in November 1903 against Colombia had resulted in Panama becoming an independent republic. The United States quickly recognized the new nation and was now pushing through a treaty that would allow it to build the Panama Canal. The streets were full of people discussing this momentous event and the canal construction plans.

Their stop in Panama lasted four nights before they continued in a small sailing vessel to South America. The first stop would be Ecuador. Harriet enjoyed seeing the remainder of the Central American coast, but was eager for her first glimpse of South America. When the small boat finally reached the equator, Harriet was surprised. It was cold. The wind was blowing so hard Harriet had to run back to her cabin for warmer clothes.

Their stay in Guayaquil, Ecuador, was short, and the remainder of February was spent at sea and at small ports. On March 2, they arrived in Callao, Peru. From here they planned to journey to Lima for the month of March.

Throughout her first two months of the trip, Harriet wrote in her journal and also wrote several long letters home. These "home letters" became the basis for future articles. In them she minutely described every detail of their travels, from the colors of native clothing to what they ate for dinner.

Lima was cosmopolitan with its museums, theaters, shops. On their third day in the Peruvian capital, a "great" earthquake occurred at five in the morning as they slept. When the thunderous effect was over, they went into the streets to see

Harriet seemed "more at home in a drawing room than leading the rugged life of an explorer."

statues overturned and buildings in shambles.

To learn the culture, they explored museums as well as talked to people. This desire to meet the citizens was typical of the Adams. They respected the natives and treated them as equals.

They left Lima on March 26, boarding another ship in Callao. Again, Harriet became extremely seasick. The sea breeze and some tea and broth revived her. The port of Mollendo, Peru, was their destination. From there they traveled to Arequipa to begin acclimatizing themselves to the altitude, preparing for their eventual journey into the Andes.

To begin their high altitude trip, they journeyed to La Paz, Bolivia. Once finished in La Paz, they would return by lake and take the railroad to Tirapata, beginning their saddle trip of one thousand miles across the Andes.

Bolivia had only recently become accessible to the outside world by railroad. Few people had traveled there. The local color had not been marred by modern civilization, which Harriet described as a "despoiler."

Traveling to La Paz meant a trip on the second highest railroad in the world, connecting Mollendo with Lake Titicaca, the highest lake on earth. One hundred and twenty miles long and sixty miles wide at an elevation of 12,500 feet, Lake Titicaca was truly a "Lake of the Clouds." When they boarded a small steamer to cross the lake, Harriet felt the effects of the high altitude. It felt as if she had a weight on her chest suffocating her lungs. The couple adjusted during the two nights spent on the lake before boarding the train to La Paz.

Frank Adams became fascinated with Harriet the first time he saw her.

Alighting from the train at Alto La Paz, Harriet looked in vain for the city. A railway station and three old-fashioned stage coaches awaiting city-bound passengers were the only indications of civilization. On either side of the track a dreary brown plain seemed to stretch unbroken to the snowy range of the Andes. Not a single house or hut was in sight. It was bitterly cold; Alto La Paz was 13,000 feet above the sea.

"But where is La Paz de Ayacucho, the metropolis of Bolivia?" she asked Frank.

"I'm sure it's close," he said, looking for their luggage.

While Frank attended the luggage, she walked along the road to keep warm. Suddenly, she found herself on the brink of a deep canyon not visible from the station platform. Far below, in the narrow valley, lay a red-roofed city accessed by a steep, serpentine wagon-road.

Harriet's breath was taken away by La Paz. It was a view she would remember for the rest of her life.

Leaving the lofty railroad station, their stage driver lashed his mules into a gallop. Harriet sat on top of the coach, expecting a splendid view. She held fast to the seat's railing. They dashed down the steep, zigzag road but missed the scenery because the view was obscured by dust the entire trip.

They stayed in a hotel where the floors were red tile, the ceiling white plaster with huge wooden beams. Harriet and Frank could stand on the narrow balcony and watch passing natives. She felt it was "a play staged and costumed by a master hand . . . The curtain was rung up in the early morning, distant trumpeters announcing the prologue."

Harriet bought her broad-brimmed "Merry Widow" hat in the Peruvian highlands.

Harriet threw on her pink dressing gown and rushed to watch the Bolivian regimental band marching down the hill. For a half hour the brilliantly uniformed soldiers played in the plaza opposite their windows. As the soldiers marched away, the water-carriers gathered by the fountain in the center of the plaza to fill the immense copper jars carried on their backs. These were full-blooded Aymaras, descendants of a people conquered by the Incas.

The Adamses took time out to eat breakfast, then it was back to the balcony for more entertainment. Llama drivers shouted as they urged their flocks downhill. Harriet enjoyed the way the llamas carried their heads with a regal air of indifference. Often they wore brightly colored red and yellow ear ribbons; small ornamental bags hung about their necks.

The delights of La Paz finally had to be left behind. The return voyage across the lake was rough and disagreeable. A number of passengers suffered from seasickness or from *soroche*, altitude sickness.

Armed with their excellent Spanish and complete maps of the valleys and the Andes region, Harriet and Frank were ready to start their inland journey. Frank's contract with the Inca Mining and Rubber Company required the inspection of mines in remote areas on the Andes eastern slope. To accomplish their journey they needed horses, pack animals and, whenever possible, a guide. While in Tirapata they met Danny, an English naturalist who decided to travel with them, and Pedro, who would be their guide.

During their ascent of the Andes, Harriet discovered not

only humans but animals could succumb to *soroche*. When she saw evidences of it in her mule, she whipped out her smelling salts (always carried by women in that era) and applied it to the mule's nose. Frank laughed heartily, but her experiment worked. Ever after, she used her bottle with success whenever the mules appeared sick.

The couple planned to live as the natives, so they started out with only what they could carry in saddlebags. Sleeping conditions were either on the dirt floors of huts or in the open. They ate what the natives ate.

When they reached the 17,000 foot Pass of Aricoma, the view was overwhelming. The plans called for a swift descent down the eastern Andes and into the tributaries of the Amazon River. Harriet's excitement was contagious. Frank and Danny knew she could manage the difficult descent—and so did Harriet.

"I managed on all my trips to get along well; and I've wondered why men have so absolutely monopolized the field of exploration," she said later. "Why did women never go to the Arctic, try for one pole or the other, or invade Africa, Tibet or unknown wildernesses? I've never found my sex a hinderment; never faced a difficulty which a woman, as well as a man, could not surmount; never felt a fear of danger; never lacked courage to protect myself. I've been in tight places, have seen harrowing things."

VAMPIRE BATS AND UNMAPPED REGIONS

The Adamses were deep in the jungle east of the Andes, traveling with two comrades and a guide. Toward evening they stopped when they discovered a hut in the limbs of a tree. The hut was made from the fan-like leaves of the palmetto tree. Exhausted from a day of jungle travel, where each step had to be cleared by machete, they decided to eat on the ground and sleep in the shelter. Harriet lit an alcohol lamp and made a soup of pulverized peas and tea.

After dinner the men played cards. They soon discovered the lit candle attracted so many insects they couldn't see their cards, so they prepared for sleep. Harriet slept on a raised platform, the four men were on the floor.

Before going to sleep, Harriet wrote in her journal about the creakings and uncanny noises coming from the jungle outside the hut: "I suppose those sounds come from jaguars playing tag about the house," she wrote. It was hard to go to sleep in the noisy woods. Finally, exhaustion overcame her.

She awoke suddenly, conscious of a strange sound inside the hut. It was like the purring of a hundred cats. The black air about her seemed to be moving—yet she saw nothing. Then she distinctly heard the sound of swiftly beating wings and wanted to rise. But she was powerless, as though hypnotized and under the spell of the soothing purring sounds. In a semi-stupor she lay there. Then she saw black creatures appear and disappear, again and again. Shaking with fear, she instinctively drew the thick veil over her face and drifted into unconsciousness.

When the morning's sunlight poured through the hut's door, Harriet discovered that the men on the floor had bloody wounds in their throats, breasts and necks. They were breathing with difficulty. Finally, one of the men, a doctor, drank some brandy and began to revive.

"Tell me—what were they?" Harriet asked.

"Vampires," he said grimly.

"Vampires?"

"Yes, natives say they infest whole stretches of this forest—that there are vampire bats," the doctor said. "We have got among them. When they made their attack on us, they descended and poised over their victim. Swiftly beating their wings, they produced a sound resembling the purring of a cat, which seemed to have a hypnotic quality and soothed a person or animal into profound slumber. Then they descended upon our exposed throats and shaved or scratched away the skin with their sharp, incisive teeth." Having drawn her veil, Harriet had escaped harm.

Harriet medicated and bandaged the bitten men. Then they ate some breakfast and descended the rope ladder. On the ground lay one of their mules, dead. The others were weak. Later the doctor pointed to a dead tree.

"Do you want to see the vampires?" He fired a shot into the tree. Huge bats swarmed, measuring eighteen to twenty-eight inches from tip to tip of their wings.

The remainder of the time in the forest they covered their faces when they slept. They weren't attacked again, but other treacheries lay ahead.

This vampire adventure occured when Harriet and Frank traveled from the "Roof of the Western World"—the summit of the Andes—to an area known as "the inside"—an impenetrable jungle stretching three thousand miles from the Andes to the Atlantic.

The day before the downward journey, the Adams had traveled over fifty miles. They crossed the Peruvian Cordillera, a desolate highland at an elevation of 17,000 feet, enduring a "terrible" road and freezing snowstorm during the fourteen-hour journey.

Slowly, they descended into a "cavern of mist"—four travelers, four saddle horses, and one pack mule. Rifles hung from the pommels of the saddles; blankets and cameras were strapped behind, and saddle bags bulged with necessities for the wild.

Then they slid—down one of the steepest, slipperiest trails Harriet had ever seen. The trail took them into the Aganlani Canyon, one of the most beautiful places in the world. But, beautiful as it was, she was cold and exhausted. Mist enshrouded each animal and obscured the rider ahead. Rain fell in torrents, penetrating the heaviest rain gear. Harriet's tired white horse tripped over rolling boulders and pitched her head over heels into a steam. There she lay, too tired to move, until the men came to the rescue.

They had started at dawn to cross the Andes, hoping to avoid the daily noon snowstorm. Beginning at Crucero, a tiny native hamlet in Southern Peru, it was three miles above sea level and extremely cold. Harriet had piled on a heavy sweater, a long khaki coat and a tattered woolen blanket with a hole in the center for her head over her corduroy suit. She also wore long woolen stockings over high boots, a red flannel cap with ear flaps under her sombrero and two pairs of mittens. Hardly "a picture of the personification of grace," Harriet said to Frank.

All that clothing became soaked. Down they slipped, through water torrents spilling over rocks. By dusk they had dropped five thousand feet. Ahead was a mud-walled, thatch-roofed settlement straggling along both sides of the stream.

Quichua Indians manned this frontier outpost, their main villages being in the Peruvian highlands. Not one Indian was visible—no one welcomed them. Pedro, their native guide, stopped to warm himself and kept the pack animal with him. The remaining three continued down the canyon, knowing they would not be welcome in the village.

At this point the trail, never over thirty inches wide, left the river and climbed the cliff. It wound along a stony ledge with a sheer drop of a thousand feet to the canyon below, with projecting crags and sharp turns. Harriet regretted using a sidesaddle. Her feet hung over the yawning chasm. Dimly, she saw a faint, silvery thread winding far below in the mist—the river serpentining its way through the canyon. Not until midnight did the three adventurers find a hut on the edge of the forest. They had spent nineteen hours in the saddle.

The hut was owned by an American mining company. An American man stayed there to oversee incoming provisions and mail, and outgoing gold and mail. At this point Danny, the naturalist, left them, excited about his search for beautifully opalescent butterflies.

Pedro did not show up the first night, nor the next morning. They assumed he had lingered in the village and would overtake them later in the day. Reluctantly, they decided to proceed by themselves. The American gave them directions: "Follow the river. And be sure to look for the new trail at the foot of the canyon; I hear there's been a landslide on the old one."

Their tortuous path, cut out of rock on the side of a gorge, crossed and recrossed the canyon by swinging bridges hung on cables. The bridges were only three feet wide without railings, and swayed precariously as they rode over them. Harriet wanted to dismount and walk across when they came to a bridge, but could not. There was no room to place her feet.

Despite the danger, fatigue, and low provisions, the canyon was enchanting. Its walls were luxuriant greenery framing silvery waterfalls. Pink and white begonias as large as bushes and giant ferns grew beside the trail. They looked down on waving palms, huge orchid trees and iridescent butterflies.

Caribbean Sea

Cartagena•

Atlantic Ocean

VENEZUELA

• Bogota
COLOMBIA
• Cali

British
Dutch
French
GUIANA

• Quito
ECUADOR
Cuenca•
Iquitos•

ANDES

AMAZON RIVER

PERU

BRAZIL

Lima•
Cuzco•
BOLIVIA
Arequipa•
Lake Titicaca
• La Paz

PARAGUAY

CHILE

ANDES

ARGENTINA

Valparaiso•
Santiago•

URUGUAY

• Rio de Janeiro

Pacific
Ocean

South America in 1905

Cape Horn

In the afternoon Harriet called out, "This is the thirteenth bridge. Maybe it's the unlucky one!" At that moment a train of llamas came toward them across the chasm. Frank slipped off his horse and dragged Harriet over her pony's head. They couldn't meet the group head-on. The trail was too narrow. All they could do was run to the widest place in sight and flatten themselves against the wall.

Over the swaying bridge came the llamas, heads erect, curious eyes wandering. Following were two Indian drivers calling, "Buss-ss-ss." This hissing cry caused the llamas to prick up their ears and walk faster. When the animals saw the Adamses, they panicked. They scrambled past, trembling with fear. One golden-brown llama made a misstep, struck another llama in his fall, and they both went over the brink.

The picture of this catastrophe haunted Harriet for days.

Later, the daily storm drenched Harriet and Frank. Again, they were soaking wet and miserable. As night approached, they were stumbling along a rock ledge in a downpour, leading their horses through the darkness. Huge rocks fell about them. The earth seemed to slip beneath their feet. Water rushed down the hollow road and the horses were almost swept from their feet.

To keep their spirits up, Frank began to sing "Oh, ain't it a shame, a measly shame, to keep us waiting, out in the rain." Harriet laughed, clutching the reins.

At nine o'clock they dismounted. It was pitch black. Frank went ahead, leading his horse, followed by Harriet. The trail narrowed to a one-foot width. They put their backs against the rocks and held on with both hands. Then it dawned on them. They had taken the old trail with the landslide. Desperately, they turned to go back, but Harriet's horse could not turn on the narrow trail. They crept on hands and knees. The horses were as cautious as the humans.

The rain fell in torrents and lightning flashed. In the canyon below rushed furious rain-swollen waters.

Suddenly, an avalanche of earth and stones, loosened by the rain, descended from above. Harriet tried to secure herself as rocks and stones struck her. As quickly as it arrived, the avalanche disappeared down the mountain side.

"This is death," Harriet said to Frank. "We can't go on."

He encouraged her, praising her as they continued to creep forward. Finally, they reached the bottom of the canyon, expecting to find a bridge. The bridge had washed away. Total discouragement overtook them. They could do nothing but try to sleep in this wet, miserable place. Throughout the night they were tortured by hordes mosquitoes.

When the sun arose they discovered everything in the saddle bags was soaked. Only a dozen dry malted-milk tablets had escaped the deluge. Venturing down to the river, all that remained of the old bridge was one log. Food, dry clothing and shelter were on the other side of the river—they had to risk the log.

Harriet and Frank realized the horses could not brave the river and would have to remain behind. They began what she called "their circus act on the long, slippery log, high above the roaring river."

Frank improvised a line from bridles and fastened it around Harriet's waist. Then he held on to it while she lay flat and pulled herself across, inch by inch. In mid-current she became so dizzy she almost lost hold.

More rocky trails and swollen streams followed. In one stream Harriet lost her footing and Frank had to pull her out by her hair. When she was safe, Harriet pulled out a small mirror and jokingly primped.

Through it all Harriet hung on to three possessions tied in her sombrero—her journal wrapped in oilskin, a necktie that a mother in California had crocheted for her son living at the far Andean mine, and a jar of cold cream.

When they finally reached the Ianambari River, their journey was almost over. It had taken them five days to reach the mines, from April 18 to April 23, 1904.

The mining company had gone to great expense to entice Americans to work at Santo Domingo, offering several "luxuries." Harriet enjoyed a wonderful soak in a porcelain-lined bathtub, followed by an excellent meal. They even had electric lights—amazing conveniences in an isolated outpost.

When preparing for this trip, Harriet felt these isolated workers would like to see a woman dressed in American garb. Toward this end she packed a few simple cotton shirtwaist dresses in a rubber bag—which never arrived. Her costume instead, until her corduroy suit dried, was the mine doctor's bathrobe, the superintendent's underwear and an engineer's slippers. Her hair hung in a braid because she had lost all her hairpins.

Harriet enjoyed the proud walk and grace of the llamas.

After a six-day rest, Harriet and Frank were ready to venture into the "inside country," a region which had thrilled Harriet when she read about it in *The Big Geography*. Few of the rivers had names as yet, the miners told them. In fact, all of the country beyond the mine was marked "unexplored" on the Peruvian maps. It was rumored to be peopled by savage natives who had seen few white men and no white women.

The men at the mine shook their heads at the thought of a woman undertaking this journey. The Adamses were joined by the mine's doctor and an engineer. A new guide was added along with fresh horses and a sturdy cargo mule. They all were armed, as they would depend on game for food.

As the group started the trip, they came to a spot where they could look back on the ranges they had crossed. Far in the distance gleamed the towering snow peaks of the highest range of the Andes. Then they turned toward their trail and saw, as on a raised map, the long, winding canyon through which they were to descend to the plain.

The group left their horses at a rubber camp and made the next part of their journey on foot. It was especially difficult traveling for Harriet. They hacked and forced their way through the brush, feet sinking in the trail's soft mud.

Finally, they reached the Peruvian frontier post of Puerto Candamo—a few shacks perched at the meeting of two navigable rivers. Here a homesick young captain, Mr. Martinez, and eight soldiers were stationed. The captain was from Lima, Peru, and had been in this outpost three years. He was thrilled by the group's canned goods after living on game, yucca and plantain. That night they had a marvelous banquet—combining all their food stuffs into a delectable meal.

Harriet and Frank had descended from seventeen thousand feet in the Andes to twelve hundred feet above sea level. Now they ventured into the land of the Chunchos, a powerful tribe who had remained unconquered by the Incas. Fortunately, the previous white explorers had been kind, so the Chunchos were inclined to be friendly. Also, when a solitary white man arrived with a "chinani" as they called a woman, the wilderness people regarded it as a friendly call.

A canoe ride took them to La Union, their final destination in the "inside," where they stayed for two nights, resting and even swimming in the river. Harriet had become the first woman to travel from La Union to West River

The return to Santo Domingo took two days. While Frank began his inspection of the mines, Harriet enjoyed some brief leisure time. She mailed several "home" letters, including twenty-two photographs.

After eleven days at Santo Domingo, the Adamses began their return to the Andean highlands. Harriet almost hated to leave these luxuries, knowing what lay ahead on the trail. Her journey "inside" had been one of the triumphs of her life.

In later years she would recall this epic journey: "You may wonder how I managed in the wilds with scanty equipment. I relied on Dame nature. She has vine-screened bathtubs in the river, soft leaves for towels and bark for soap in the forest. It is amazing how well groomed one can be, with care, even without the luxuries of civilization. Clothes become tattered, and shoes have a most annoying habit of wearing out; but the air and the sunlight, and the adventure and romance of exploration are full compensation to some of us for discomfort, hardship and danger.

"Since the expedition into the inside country of Peru we have reached many other unmapped regions where I have been the first white woman, yet no other land has been so dear to me... the greatest lure lies in that enchanting forest country on the other side of the Andes."

THE OLD INCA HIGHWAY

The return trip up the Andes was both treacherous and exhausting. They climbed higher and higher, mile after painful mile. In later years Harriet was certain the strenuous climb had strained the valves in her heart. At fifteen-thousand feet they were caught in a driving blizzard that battered them with snow and freezing wind. Harriet became faint, wobbled, and fell off her horse. Frank lifted her to a soft spot on the ground. "It was a bare mountain side," said Harriet later, "without possibility of refuge or help. Only a miracle could save us, it seemed."

They discovered they were not alone. A herd of llamas stood down the mountain side. The group stumbled down to the fluffy animals, who took no notice of them. "Probably they never had seen human beings before," said Frank later. The llamas allowed them to creep in and nestle close. Harriet pillowed her head on the warm fur of one and placed her feet under the body of another. The next morning she told Frank, "I slept warm and comfortable."

On the outward journey from the jungle, Harriet and Frank

lost their way. Leaving the pass of Aricoma, they mistakenly turned toward the Poto mine. Each night seemed colder than the one before. Ice froze in Harriet's hair; tears came to her eyes; her lids froze together.

Morning sun and hot tea revived them. Stumbling into Poto, they found a house and a friendly host. However, at the seventeen-thousand feet altitude, Harriet did not feel like eating. Frank also suffered from the altitude, as well as with aches from time in the saddle. They fell into a hard bed, grateful for rest.

After a two-day rest at Poto, they were eager to leave the cold weather. The end of May was the Andean wintertime, and each day felt colder than the last. Yet they could not lose their nerve. Four days over the pampa would take them to Tirapata and a real bed in a hotel.

In Tirapata, after four days rest, they decided to hire a vehicle to travel to the ancient city of Cuzco. Then they could stop wherever they wanted to view scenery, natives and ancient ruins. When Harriet saw their private transportation, she wasn't happy. A rickety mule-pulled cart held Harriet, Frank and their sullen driver.

The Old Inca Highway had been used since before the Spanish conquest and was worn by the feet of many pilgrims, llama trains, and varied travelers. Each mile moved them closer to the past. Finally they reached Cuzco. Seeing the city was the culmination of a childhood dream for Harriet. She gazed down on the old town nestled at one end of a golden valley. Moorish designed buildings had slanting roofs of

Visiting Cuzco was the culmination of a childhood dream for Harriet.

reddish-brown tile. Picturesque streams flowed through the streets and the open plazas. Unfortunately, these streams turned out to be, on closer inspection, open sewers which Harriet said "rival Constantinople in unpleasant odors—in fact, I believe Cuzco holds the world's record."

Vehicles were not allowed in the city. Instead, burros and llamas were everywhere. Several moved along the streets, hidden by the bundles they carried.

Harriet would never forget her entrance into Cuzco. They ported innumerable bags, boxes and cameras down the rock road into town, hoping to find adequate lodging. When they paid only one dollar each for room and board per day they were a little suspicious.

Their suspicions were well-founded. The courtyard was strewn with rubbish, and their room had canvas partition walls extending only halfway to the ceiling. The room was dirty and cold. But they did not complain; the beautiful town more than compensated for their inconvenience.

Cuzco was as interesting and picturesque as Harriet had imagined. In the morning they were served *desayuno*—a chocolate made from native cocoa and enhanced with a dash of cinnamon. Breakfast (*almuerzo*) was served at 11:30 a.m. and dinner (*comida*) at 6 p.m. They made daily trips to the market to buy tropical fruits from the lowlands.

The Quichuas interested Harriet more than any other native people. They were gentle, fond of one another, patient and uncomplaining. Fascinated by their beautiful and expressive language, she soon learned it. Harriet took photo after photo of the Quichuas, showing their life in the town and rural areas. Women in bright dress, children with bare feet, llama herdsman in wide-brimmed hat continually caught her eye.

From Cuzco, Harriet and Frank decided to travel north to the Valley of Yucay. This would be a ten-day trip through areas seldom seen by outsiders. Starting out, they wondered where the valley could be hidden. Then they reached the edge of the plateau and saw the canyon-like valley four thousand feet below. Harriet remembered her first glimpse of California's Yosemite Valley. Like the Yosemite, steep walls lined the Yucay. However, instead of waterfalls, these walls were covered with graceful terraces.

Their descent into Yucay by a narrow, winding trail put Harriet into an exalted mood. She imagined she was a Quichua princess carried to the beautiful summer palace of her father, the Inca. Then her tired horse stumbled, and she abruptly returned to reality. She was only a dusty little Andean traveler.

A posada (small inn) was found in the village of Urubamba. The Admas felt it broke all records for uncleanliness. However, they couldn't complain. They only paid seventy cents for bed, a day's board and fodder for their animals.

From Urubamba, they rode down the valley over a trail following a winding river. Passing through peaceful villages, they came upon surviving terraces and moss-hung ruins. The Fortress of Ollantyatambo guarded the lower entrance of Yucay. Harriet never ceased marveling at the enormous rocks that had been carried across the great mountain heights from far-away quarries.

No rooms were available when they visited Ollantyatambo. While they enjoyed the historic sites and scenic vistas, they slept in less than ideal places—a room where maize was spread to dry, a filthy room of a hospitable home owner, and the offices of the village prefect. Perhaps their most unusual experience was in the small town of Pisac. The gobernador, or chief magistrate, offered his hospitality. However, he had no extra beds in his house so they slept on the dining-room table. At three in the morning they were awakened by the crowing of roosters. They found the family's pet fighting cocks were tied to the table legs. Harriet called it the "Peruvian alarm clock!"

Travel through the highlands was long and difficult, with little food and less water. The rivers and brooks were polluted by sewage. They met few travelers except the highland Indians. "Even the Spanish colonial days have faded," she said to Frank. "We are in the old Peru before the conquerors arrived."

By July, Harriet and Frank were traveling toward the coast. When they again reached Arequipa, they decided to climb Mt. Misti, a 19,200-foot peak. Harriet told Frank, "We are in the neighborhood. It would be a shame not to go up." She had climbed many peaks in the Sierra Nevada mountains, so didn't think this would be a challenge.

Mt. Misti was a cold and arduous trail ride. The travellers rode for an hour after dark. Even after finding a hut, they were cold in their sleeping bags. Rats ran around all night, the wind howled and forks of lightning split the sky around them.

The Quichuas interested Harriet more than any other native people.

Sunrise was worth all the pain. As they rode to the summit on the lava trail, Harriet could feel her heart beating from both the altitude and the sheer glory of the view. When they reached the top she had the most wonderful and comprehensive view, another experience she would treasure.

Much of the remaining South American trip in 1904 was by boat—cattle boat, sailing vessel, canoe, even a whaling vessel. From the highlands, Harriet and Frank returned to the Peruvian coast and sailed south to Chile.

They reached Valpariso, Chile, on August 17 and stayed a month before journeying inland to Santiago, the capital. Several train and boat rides later they arrived at Harriet's favorite Chilean city, Valdivia, a German settlement. She considered it one of the loveliest cities on the continent. Their base city during this time in Southern Chile was Corral.

Harriet and Frank took a cattle boat and a whaling vessel through the Strait of Magellan. Later they called it "some of the finest scenery in the world." But at the time Harriet fended off her old traveller's demon—seasickness. The boat rocked until Harriet felt like she couldn't stand it. The wind blew like a gale, cold and miserable—then the magnificently high glaciers came into view, coming right down to the sea.

Another goal was met—they reached the southernmost tip of South America. Here they found a ship bound for Buenos Aires. During the voyage, the ship docked in small harbors and they were able to explore many native towns.

They decided to spend time in Buenos Aires before beginning their next adventure, an exploration of the vast Amazon jungle. The Andean journey had been difficult, but Harriet and Frank had no regrets about the severe traveling conditions. "To know a country and a people, one must leave the highway and live near to Nature," Harriet wrote later. "We traveled much in the saddle on this great elevated plateau—over a thousand miles on a single journey—and gradually my viewpoint changed. I started as an outsider, having little real sympathy for the Quichuas and Aymaras, little understanding of the history and environment which has made them the sullen, lifeless folk they are. In time I grew, through study and observation, but more through sharing the life . . . and find . . . my greatest heart interest lies in the highlands of Peru and Bolivia."

JUNGLE DEPTHS AND ISLAND BLISS

Harriet and Frank enjoyed their time in Buenos Aires. The city, one of the largest in South America, impressed them with its wide boulevards, bustling port, and the residents' cosmopolitan nature.

After resting, the Adamses were ready to travel again. Frank wanted to see Argentina from Patagonia to Buenos Aires. They returned by ship to southern Argentina in early 1905 and hired horses and guides so they could ride the length of the country. Harriet was at home in the saddle but unprepared for the wind, which blew "as I have never seen it blow anywhere else in my life." It was impossible to keep a hat on, so she finally decided to let her hair stream free.

Before leaving Buenos Aires, they mapped out a route to the Matto Grosso country of Brazil. This was the richest province of the country, full of diamond and gold mines. Frank could finance their trip by inspecting the mines.

From Buenos Aires they sailed on a steamer up the La Plata until it branched into the Parana River and eventually flowed into the Paraguay. The river journey ended on the Upper

Paraguay in Bolivia. Harriet was appalled by boa constrictors on the river. The snakes were everywhere—even hanging in the paddle wheels of the steamer where they were ground up. Upon reaching Eastern Bolivia, they switched back to horses. They rode horseback in Matto Grosso and throughout Paraguay.

After inspecting mines in Paraguay, they sailed the Upper Parana River to Igauzu Falls on the Brazilian-Argentine border. They had heard that these falls were some of the most spectacular in the world. Nearly two miles in width, there were over 137 distinct falls. Harriet took photos from every angle, from sunrise to sunset.

Although reluctant to leave, Harriet and Frank had further plans. They visited Uruguay and its capital Montevideo, then sailed north along the coast of Brazil. Again they traveled in small ships, exploring coastal ports along the way.

Rio de Janeiro was a welcome contrast from the primitive living conditions they had experienced on the trip. Calling it a "handsome city with a wonderful harbor," they stayed long enough to enjoy its civilized comforts before forging onward to the Amazon.

Harriet found the mouth of the Amazon River disappointing. "It looks more like a wide and dirty brown lake flowing into the blue sea than a river," she told Frank. They began their westward Amazon journey on steamers with passengers. By the time they arrived at the branches and tributaries, they were in canoes. Alligators lined the shore. As often as possible, they would stop in huts to view the home life of the natives and study their customs. It took three months to explore the Amazon forest.

It was during this three months that Harriet had one of the most frightening episodes of her life. As she explained it: "I was nearly eaten alive, but not by animals."

Harriet, Frank, and three others were lost and decided to stop for the night and pitch tent beside a large cypress tree in a clearing in the dense jungle. Harriet's bed was a hammock overhung with a thick insect net. As she drifted off to sleep, she thought she saw a huge arm near the spot where Frank was sleeping. Suddenly, she heard a gurgling noise. At the same moment, she felt a numbness in her feet. She screamed. The men awoke and discovered the guide entangled in the coils of a tree's tendrils! Frank and the men cut the tendrils from the guide's body. The guide was almost crushed, and so weakened he had to stop at the next settlement.

The cypress was encircled by a "strangler fig" tree, so-called because it sent out long, deadly tendrils that wrapped around objects and crushed them. In Harriet's imagination, they had narrowly escaped an unusual, horrifying death!

Reluctantly, they returned to the Amazon's mouth, this time at its northern terminus. They had to wait for transportation. The North Brazilian coast was not a normal sailing route. Finally, they found a captain who agreed to take them to Cayenne, French Guiana. But the captain deserted them at a port in northern Brazil with no transportation in sight. Frank searched for a ship or other type of vehicle, with no success. They decided to continue to French Guiana on horseback.

This photo by Harriet was called "River Enclosed Paraguay" when first published in *National Geographic Magazine.*

En-route to Guiana, Harriet and Frank spent three months in the forests with the Indians and the Bosch Negroes. The arduous trip ended on the Oyapoc river, the boundary between Brazil and French Guiana. Again they navigated the length of this river, stopping in Indian huts. Harriet observed the home life of the natives and documented their customs.

Harriet almost died during this part of the journey after eating a fowl killed with a poisoned-tipped arrow. A huron she had made a pet died after eating the same meat. For twenty-four hours she hovered close to death. Civilization and medicine were beyond reach. After a week, she was able to resume the journey. A sailing vessel came to the village to take them back to civilization. French Guiana seemed small after the immensity of Brazil. They traveled by canoe and sailing vessel, up one river, down another, visiting native villages, exploring the jungle, tracking wildlife.

Harriet was the first woman to journey from the Amazon river to Cayenne, French Guiana. By this time, she noted in her journal on January 9, 1906, it had been two years since they had left San Francisco. This was a long time—and on that particular day Harriet said, "life is *triste* (sad)." She also wrote her fifty-first "home" letter.

Her spirits revived when they journeyed to Curacao, a beautiful tropical island in the Caribbean, where they swam— Harriet in the "ladies' tank and Frank in the men's." They rested and Harriet prepared articles and lectures for their return home. Curacao was more home-like than any place they had seen since California.

Colombia was their final South American destination. Harriet was delighted with Cartagena, calling it the second most wonderful ancient city visited (after Cuzco). The entire month of April she and Frank poked into old ruins, met the people, and prepared more lectures. On April 29, 1906, they returned to Panama. Traveling by trail and canoe across the Isthmus, they were fascinated by the changes in two years as the construction of the Panama Canal continued. Then they caught a train to Panama City, "their circuit of South America completed."

As Harriet and Frank stood on a high point overlooking the Pacific Ocean and gazed back on the continent they had traversed together, their emotions rose up and they could not speak. Hardships, dangers, and discomforts were forgotten in that moment of accomplishment. They had completed a journey made by only a few people—and none of them before had been a woman.

TELLING THE SOUTH AMERICA TALE

One barrier stood between Harriet and Frank's plans to travel—money. While Frank's expertise as an engineer paid for their trip to Mexico and their expedition through Central and South America, returning to the United States halted this income flow. It would be necessary to find a way to finance future trips, and the best way to do this was to move to a larger city and try to find people willing to pay them for their skills. On May 16, 1906, Harriet and Frank watched the New York skyline come into view as they sailed into the harbor.

Frank's stay in New York City was brief. With his experience in Latin America he easily found a job with the Bureau of American Republics (Pan American Union) as an editor. His home base would be Washington, D. C. Harriet hesitated. She did not want to settle down as a housewife.

What could Harriet do after all those adventures? How could she earn extra money to continue traveling? The answer was not long in coming.

Harriet had kept a complete journal of the Central and South American journey, written over fifty detailed "home" letters to her family, and had taken three thousand photos and dozens of motion picture rolls. Would other people be interested in what she had seen?

She sent a letter to Gilbert Grosvenor, president of the National Geographic Society, summarizing her travel in Latin America and offering to lecture to the society. Grosvenor was entranced by the vividly-worded circular she enclosed with the letter. The short anecdotes and photographs intrigued him. He invited her to Washington to meet.

Harriet selected slides to illustrate her lecture technique, and practiced telling about the exciting travel incidents. She easily won Grosvenor's confidence. He agreed to have her lecture before the National Geographic Society in late 1906.

Harriet's interview with Grosvenor led to a lifetime friendship. She often asked his advice while attempting to interest him in ideas for articles. She worked with the National Geographic Society for nearly thirty years. She published two articles in _National Geographic Magazine_ in 1907, and in the years ahead she had as many as three published annually.

Harriet's first lecture to the society was enthusiastically received. Members were charmed by this petite woman describing adventures undertaken by few men. Her lecture style was warm and descriptive. She had a sense of drama and often wore dramatic red gowns to compliment her dark brown hair and dark eyes. Reporters usually referred to her as "this demure young woman in the startling red velvet gown."

The photographs taken by Frank and Harriet added another dramatic element. They were the first people in the United

States to use natural color photography professionally in slide illustration. Thus, her lectures were enhanced both by stereopticon slides and motion pictures.

Harriet soon began traveling the country giving her lectures. One of Harriet's most exciting appearances was in her hometown of Stockton on October 29, 1907. She spoke at the Yosemite Theater, the same place Frank managed in 1895. The audience that came out to hear her was larger than the capacity of the theater. When Harriet stepped onto the stage she was given a great ovation. Friends and acquaintances had read of her achievements as an explorer, her daring and her bravery. Stocktonians were proud and admiring of their "hometown" girl.

Lecturing became a way of life for Harriet. Other educational groups, in addition to the National Geographic Society, sponsored her lectures, including the Carnegie Lyceum, the Pan American Union, and the Vassar Lecture Series. Audiences never tired of her stories of exotic lands and people, spine-tingling escapes, and hardships endured despite fatigue, danger and hunger.

Payment for her lectures began at forty dollars and increased over the years to six hundred dollars. Fees for her articles (she wrote twenty-two for *National Geographic*) started at forty dollars and increased to six hundred dollars. On one occasion she received a thousand dollars for an article, far more money than Frank was earning monthly.

Organizations throughout the United States wanted Harriet to lecture. In February 1911, the delegates to the Pan-America

HARRIET CHALMERS ADAMS

The South American Traveler, will give

An Illustrated Lecture on "Peru"

AT THE Y. M. C. A. HALL

Tuesday Evening, February 26, 1907

Two Hundred Color Pictures Illustrate the Story

THE PROCEEDS OF THIS LECTURE WILL BE USED FOR THE
FURNISHING OF THE Y. M. C. A. GAME ROOM

Reserved Seats   -   -   Fifty Cents

Tickets on Sale at Hodge's Drug Store, February 19th

AN AYMARA, A TYPE OF UPPER PERU

MRS. ADAMS has recently returned from a three years' journey through South America, during which time she visited every country on the continent and many places never before seen by a white woman. In her lecture on the Land of the Incas, Mrs. Adams tells of her wonderful trip of more than a thousand miles in the saddle, when, after crossing the eastern chain of the Andes at a height of more than 17,000 feet, she reached the vast forest land of the head waters of the Amazon.

This notice announces an upcoming lecture by the newly famous traveler. Harriet took the photo during her Latin America journey.

Commercial Conference, opened by President William Howard Taft, heard this introduction: "Mrs. Adams is recognized as the foremost woman authority on our sister republics, having traveled extensively . . ."

Harriet gave a lecture on trade with Latin American countries. At the conclusion of her illustrated lecture, the audience gave her a standing ovation.

One of Harriet's greatest triumphs was her August 1911 address to the Associated Advertising Clubs of America convention. It was the first time in the organization's history that a woman took part in convention ceremonies. Timidity was never part of Harriet's vocabulary. She was well aware that she knew far more than most delegates about Latin American conditions. She opened: "I believe that Americans on the whole know comparatively little (about the Latin American republics) today." She admitted prior to her visit, she too "was very ignorant regarding them." In fact, she said, she knew so little she didn't realize Portuguese, not Spanish, was spoken in Brazil. She continued by pointing out how often exporters made this same mistake, publishing in Spanish rather than Portuguese when sending to Brazil. This, too, was useful news to several delegates.

Her knowledge of Latin American business techniques created a new demand for her expertise. She proceeded to lecture on South American business methods to groups throughout the United States.

As her fame spread, Harriet spoke at several colleges. She first lectured for students at Chautauqua Institution, Chicago,

This was the most widely used publicity photo of Harriet.

then opened the Vassar Brothers' Institute course in Poughkeepsie, New York, in 1911. Her subject, "The Andean Wonderland," was an illustrated lecture. One reporter described her colored stereopticon pictures as having "rare merit," adding that her "word pictures" were as graphic as the views on the screen. The media was mesmerized and showed their enthusiasm with comments like: "Harriet Chalmers Adams is America's greatest woman explorer. As a lecturer no one, man or woman, has a more magnetic hold over an audience than she;" and "Mrs. Adams is recognized as the foremost woman authority on our Sister Republics. The pictures thrown on the screen were nothing short of marvelous. At the close of the interesting narrative the lecturer was accorded an ovation."

Several publishers recognized the commercial value of Harriet's journal. She signed a contract with Doubleday Page and Company for a book on her travels and met with another publisher's representative to discuss others.

The final question asked by most reporters was the one easiest for Harriet to answer. "What made me do it? It might be termed the 'call of the unbeaten path.' My father was a 49er ... Some of his spirit seems to have been mine by inheritance ... Always I have felt the longing to do things which other women do not do, to see things which Mesdames Brown, Jones and Smith never see, to go, go—that's about as well as I can explain it."

It was all her audience needed to hear.

THE ROUTES OF COLUMBUS

Woman Unafraid of Rats blazed the 1910 headline. The rats in question were actually solenodons. Harriet and Frank had found and brought back specimens from a trip to Haiti and the Dominican Republic. When she arrived home, Harriet was amused by the comments and publicity.

Why the interest in the solenodon? Because the only known specimen of one was caught in Haiti years previously and had died before the captor was able to photograph it. When Harriet and Frank heard about the animal, they resolved to bring one back. After fifteen days of hard riding through Haiti's wildest mountainous country, they discovered five excellent specimens and snared them as they slept in the hollow of a tree.

They placed five solenodons in boxes for transport to the United States. Then the Adamses returned to the port and boarded their ship for New York. Once aboard, they asked the ship's carpenter to be in charge of the animals. He asked anxiously, "Do they bite?"

"I think not," Frank said.

The next day Frank was proven wrong. The carpenter's

hand had been badly torn by the solenodons. He refused to continue care for the animals so someone else was found—who always wore gloves. Harriet later insisted that the solenodon was "gentle and well-mannered." Back in the U.S. the five creatures were divided between the National Zoo at Washington, D. C. and the Bronx Park Zoo in New York City.

Finding solenodons was not the main reason the Adamses traveled in Haiti and the Dominican Republic. Harriet had long wanted to trace the movements Columbus had sailed along the coast of the island. They also decided to see the interior section of the island.

Havana, Cuba, was the first stop of the trip, on May 8, 1910. They created a sensation by arriving with five trunks, a large camera and moving picture machine, saddles, blankets, and a complete camp outfit for the horseback trip through Haiti and the Dominican Republic.

Many Cubans knew about Harriet and Frank's earlier travels and were excited to meet this famous couple. Interest centered not only on the Latin American explorations, but also on the Adamses' voice for international understanding. Before starting for Haiti, the Adamses toured Cuba. Harriet inspected churches and ancient fortifications; Frank visited mines. Their final destination was the port of Santiago where they departed for Hispaniola Island.

Hispaniola lay between Cuba and Puerto Rico, the second largest of the West Indies. Columbus discovered the island in 1492 during his first voyage. He named it "Isla Espanola" which later was shortened to Hispaniola. The first settlement,

Harriet and Frank were determined to bring a solenodon back from Haiti.

an unplanned one along what is now the north coast of Haiti, was destroyed by natives. A second settlement was made on the north coast in 1493 during Columbus' second voyage. His brother Bartholomew moved the colonists to a more healthful climate near present day Santo Domingo in 1496. It was the most important city in the Spanish colonies until gold and silver were discovered on the mainland.

Hispaniola Island was divided into the Republics of Haiti and Dominican in 1795. The Dominican Republic occupies two-thirds of the mountainous island.

First, the Adamses circumnavigated the island, touching all historic points. This material later was integrated into Harriet's lecture series. Tracing the movements of Columbus, they next visited Santo Domingo.

Then they began their horseback trip, traversing the mountains east-west. Starting at Cape Haitian in the north, they traveled to Puerto Prince, a five-day ride to the south. From there they rode up the border between the two republics one hundred miles, crossed the Dominican Republic, moved up the coast and then back across. The entire journey took seventeen days.

Only a tarantula scared them on the entire trip. Ironically, this happened while they were staying in a house. Sleeping in the home of a United States custom official, they heard a rustle in the walls. They called their host who told them it was "just a tarantula. Probably the mate of the one I killed this morning." Harriet had trouble going back to sleep.

Markets were a favorite haunt of Harriet's. She enjoyed

Harriet traveled by burro though Haiti and the Dominican Republic.

seeing the women wearing brightly colored dresses, hats or bandanas of red, blue or yellow. They also were overwhelmed by the hospitality of the people in the sparsely inhabited rural areas. There were no inns but the natives gladly shared their dwellings and food.

Harriet was impressed by the good cheer and amiability of the people. The people were just as enchanted by Harriet. They were amused at the way she rode a horse—cross-saddle rather than side-saddle like most women of that day. In the towns the people would say, "Madame rides like a boy." In the country the people were more polite and said, "Madame rides like the little priest." The country folk never failed to greet the Adamses with a "Bonjour, Monsieur. Bonjour, Madame."

Following the routes of Columbus and meeting the native people motivated Harriet to continue studying the history and original languages of the native peoples of Central and South America. She also wanted to study the manners and customs of the peasantry, descendants of the ancient Incas she had met in Peru and Bolivia.

NATIVE ORIGINS

The story in the April 11, 1914, edition of the *Washington Post* was headlined **First American Native of Asia**: "After a thorough study of the peoples along the fringe of Asia from Siberia to Sumatra in her effort to trace the original American, Mrs. Harriet Chalmers Adams, one of America's foremost women explorers, in a communication to the National Geographic Society yesterday, expressed the opinion that the Ancient 'Americ' peoples came by sea, possibly in broken stages from Asia."

Harriet had achieved headline status by presenting her theories on how the first American natives came to North America. She first became interested in tracing the Asian roots of Native Americans during her first trip to South America. To support her ideas, she traveled to the Pacific and Asia.

Harriet also wanted to study the Spanish heritage in the region. Spanish customs and speech had fascinated Harriet since her childhood in California's rich Spanish and Mexican atmosphere. After her trips to Central and South America, and to the West Indies, she decided to visit every land that had ever been possessed by Spain.

She took trips to the West Indies, once more to South America with an extended stay in Argentina, to Spain and Portugal, crossed French and Spanish Morocco from east to west and from north to south, journeyed in West and North Africa and many islands of the Atlantic and Pacific.

Most trips she made alone because Frank was busy with his own work. But a six-month trip they planned together to the Far East enthralled both of them. Among their goals was to visit the head-hunters of Luzon, to cross Moro land, to cruise the Sulu Sea, and to visit Borneo and the picturesque Sultantate of Johore, then to Japan, China, and Mongolia. The trip would end with a ride on the Trans-Siberian Railroad.

Notice went to possible clients that:

HARRIET CHALMERS ADAMS

Explorer-Lecturer

is sailing for the Far East to lecture

and gather Travel Story material.

Mrs. Adams will be available for lecture

engagements in the U.S.A.

after January 1st, 1914.

Harriet and Frank began the trip in late May 1913. They first sailed to the Hawaiian Islands. While in Hawaii they took photographs, gathered information for future presentations, and visited villages where Harriet hoped to find natives

Harriet's Asian travels took her from the tropics to the snows of Siberia.

uncontaminated by civilization. She also earned some money by lecturing about her experiences in South America.

From Hawaii they boarded another sailing ship for Japan, then sailed to the Philippines. When they landed in Manila, eager reporters greeted the Adamses. Why had they come? What would they be doing?

"Our purpose," Harriet said, "is to gain knowledge of the Philippines, not to dispense it at this early date." In other words, no lectures would be given during the initial three-month stay. Always priding themselves on thorough preparation, the Adamses had read every available work on the islands before sailing.

Harriet found Manila's old city walls intact, with one or two exceptions. "It seems more like a Latin America city than an 'Oriental' one," she commented to Frank.

Then they were off to the islands of Luzon, Ceub, Mindanao, Sulu, and Borneo. They also touched on British Malay and visited Singapore. The Philippine trip completed Harriet's "Castillian chain," travels in search of Spanish possessions that had started with her Mexican honeymoon.

Travel was not easy in late fall, 1913. Conflict between ethnic groups of the Pacific was intense. Harriet and Frank decided the best course for them to follow would be to continue to meet the natives and to respect travel restrictions in their territories.

The head-hunting tribes of the Philippines particularly intrigued them. Harriet and Frank spent almost three months among the natives and were fascinated by the rapid change in their lives. A book, published ten years earlier, showed a Filipino head hunter band armed with spears, creeping up the mountain side. Late one day in Benquet she and Frank saw forty warriors—alert, noiseless, with spears erect. They expected the worse. Then the head man handed the Adamses a paper, explaining these natives were Ifogaos on the way to a nearby town to work on the new railroad. Harriet and Frank were embarrassed by their presumptions.

Harriet befriended a native chief who seemed quite warlike. A small skin bag was on his belt. Curious, she bargained with him to compare what was in his bag with the one she carried. He willingly emptied the contents: a long stick which he used to clean his ears, a spoon and a beetle nut box.

Harriet saw white rajahs and head hunters, tigers and pythons—the entire picturesque life on these Islands. What did she remember most? An American man of about twenty-two she met on a ship while sailing around the Philippines. He was an officer of the Philippines constabulary in charge of a district in Jolo occupied by an unsubdued tribe of Moros. When the boat arrived at his destination, the officer hopped off and waved his handkerchief in farewell. Away went his little command group of eight natives. Immediately, Harriet went to her cabin to cry, feeling there was little chance for the cheerful young man and his charges to come out alive. How pleased she was to meet him later!

En route to Singapore, they visited Borneo. Strange creatures fascinated them—toads as big as rabbits, snakes of gigantic proportions, and the orangutan. She saw a contrast

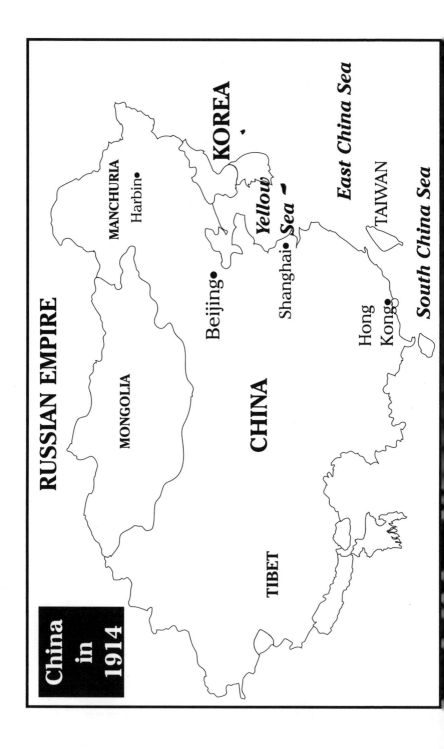

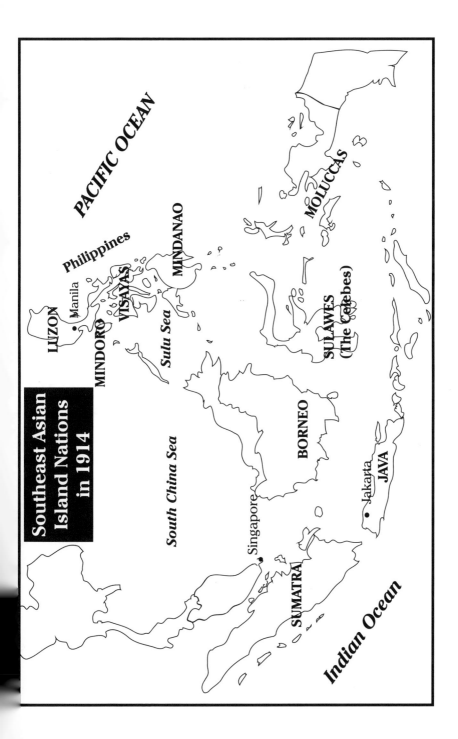

Southeast Asian Island Nations in 1914

PACIFIC OCEAN

Philippines

LUZON

Manila

MINDORO

VISAYAS

MINDANAO

Sulu Sea

MOLUCCAS

SULAWESI (The Celebes)

South China Sea

BORNEO

Singapore

SUMATRA

JAVA

Jakarta

Indian Ocean

between the fierce forest people who would creep through the
thicket after nightfall to kill, and the European colonists who
held to refinements in pagan wilds. She met pirates and
smugglers, rubber planters, tobacco growers and merchants
who made their home on the island of Borneo.

When they returned to Manila, Harriet presented a lecture
on South America at the Manila Opera House. It met with rave
reviews. Then she and Frank were off to Hong Kong.

From Hong Kong they traveled to Shanghai on the Shang-
hai-Nanking Railway, ventured to the vast Gobi desert, and
fraternized with the Mongols. They later called this trip
"traveling the fringe of Asia, from Siberia to Sumatra."

In Harbin, Manchuria, it was extremely cold. Harriet
remarked upon the heavy and valuable fur coats the public
coachmen wore. A police officer told her, "Almost every
night some coachman is shot for his skins."

As she traveled through China, Harriet became convinced
that the ancient Americ peoples came by sea (possibly in
broken stages) from Asia. She first made this announcement
in a communication to the National Geographic Society. She
expressed confidence that a closer study of the Malay, Chi-
nese, and Tibetan people would throw new light on original
Americans. In the Philippines she saw Ifugao warriors who
resembled Aymara chiefs of the Andean highlands. She took
numerous photographs to compare with her photographs of
Peruvian and Bolivian natives. From these observations she
commented: "Not only among certain Malay mountain tribes
but also in Western China was I constantly reminded of

Harriet climbs down from a horse-drawn wagon while visiting Beijing, China.

'things Americ.' . . . In olden days great war canoes were paddled by many oarsmen from one South Sea island to another. It seems likely that in this fashion men set sail from the Malay peninsula with their wives and children, food, household goods and domestic animals aboard, and aided by wind and tide, reached the promised land—some palm-fringed isle in the tropic sea."

To support her theory, Harriet had records of twenty-five small boats that apparently were blown across the Pacific. One was a Japanese fishing boat which had landed its unwilling immigrants in California two years previously.

She speculated the following groups were descendants of Asian peoples: the Incas, the Quichua people, the Mayas, the Toltecs and Aztecs, and the Pueblo Indians of the United States—especially the Zuni-Hopis. She hoped to outline all these to establish a stronger connection. Why was Harriet so adamant about this? She hoped, "to really give something of value to the world. It's our scientific interest in matters of geography, which after all includes archaeology, ethnology and many other things pertaining to life. I believe a woman's sphere is the home and if I had children I would have stayed there and spent my life trying to make a home for them. But since I have not, I hope I am trying to partly make up for it by giving something else of value."

WAR CORRESPONDENT

In the spring of 1915 Harriet booked passage on the *Lusitania*. She had picked up her tickets for the voyage before she received word of her father's sudden illness and canceled her trip. The *Lusitania* was torpedoed and sunk by the Germans on May 7. Her cancellation had been so late that her name was still on the passenger list and she was listed among the doomed passengers. Harriet's family were deluged with inquiries. Frantic telephone calls were made, telegraphs sent.

Reporters even chased the story to the home of Harriet's parents. She met the shocked reporters at the door. "I have stayed at home most of the time since I have been here," she told the reporters. "That is probably the reason I was not 'discovered' sooner. My father is ill, and during the month I have been with him, I have written seventeen magazine articles."

The next day the headline in *The Bulletin* of San Francisco, May 13, 1915, said: "**Noted Woman Changes Mind; Escapes Death.**"

Although Harriet had missed death at sea, she could not

resist the urge to be involved in the war action. By 1916, she had wrangled an assignment as a war correspondent and, equipped with credentials and photographic equipment, she sailed for France in June. Disembarking at Havre, she took the train to Paris.

A woman traveling to the war front? Unheard of, exclaimed officials. But Harriet persisted. She represented *Harpers Magazine* and also would write for *National Geographic*. An additional duty was to study war conditions under the auspices of the American Fund for French Wounded. This study provided her access to hospitals, prisons, and the front trenches.

French officials finally recognized that she was well-prepared for the hardships of war after her three years in South America, her 510-mile horseback travel in the Haitian-Dominican mountains, and her three months with Philippine head hunters. On July 18, 1916, a permit of press correspondent with the armies was issued to Harriet by the Republic of France and the minister of war. She was the only woman permitted to visit first-line trenches and to photograph French battle scenes.

Harriet marveled at her entrance passport to this military zone. She called it "a magical little yellow book which carried my photograph and the facts about my nationality, place of birth, magazine affiliation and residence at home and in Paris. It has ushered me safely past innumerable gendarmes and sentinels . . ."

Harriet was off to the battlefield. Allowed to take one

traveling companion, she selected an American girl working in Paris. Early one September morning, Harriet and her companion arrived at the Paris railway station. As they stood in line for inspection of passports, she met a young American ambulance driver on his way to the front. She noticed how his khaki uniform stood out against the mass of blue and suddenly realized, although the U.S. had not yet entered the fight, that it was only a matter of months before thousands more khaki-clad young American men joined the European War. (The United States entered World War I the following year.)

Harriet and her companion were the only women on the train. Soldiers disembarked at every station. When the American ambulance driver left them, he said, "I don't know where I'm going, but I'm on my way. I'm sure to be on the right road if I'm helping the French." Harriet felt the same and soon related this story to her readers.

Their passports were reexamined as they entered the Province of French Lorraine. Eight hours later they arrived in Nancy, the province's capital. Again, passports were scrutinized by a French official. Finally, they were allowed to walk to their hotel.

A mass of ruins across the street from the railroad station was all that remained of another once popular hotel. Other ruins lined the streets. The hotel proprietor said he had rooms, but no "cave" in case of bombardment. It had already been wrecked.

When Harriet presented her credentials to the prefect, the

executive in charge of the area, he told her the town of Nancy was only five miles from the front and was being bombarded almost daily by the German's most powerful guns. The shells came mainly at night, when there was no warning. Yet few people had left the town. Trams were running; shops were open.

Harriet interviewed people on the street, in cafes and in factories. One old woman said she was making eighty sand-bags a day for the trenches. Other women were working in munition factories and doing jobs usually reserved for men. Children still played in the great open squares and parks—until the shrill warning sound of an air raid drove citizens into the nearest house decorated with a big Lorraine cross to indicate shelter.

Once when the warning came, Harriet rushed to a base-ment shelter. An old man opened the door. She clamored down the stairway with many other people. They barely reached the bottom steps before the first crash of Titanic shells landed above. Twenty-seven people crowded into the cellar. The old man and a soldier were the only men. One little boy held a dog in his arms, and a girl of ten grasped a cage with a pet canary.

The bombardment lasted three-quarters of an hour. Harriet timed the shells by her watch, noting they fell every seven minutes. They remained in the cellar for some time after the last crash because it had sounded much nearer than the others. When they reached the streets, boys and girls were flying kites, pretending they were German planes.

Harriet said her passport to the French front of World War I was "a magical little yellow book . . ."

One of Harriet's main duties was to visit hospitals. Not only was she a correspondent but also the bearer of the American people's concern for the French and their war-torn country.

Eventually, she visited the first-line trenches of Champagne. Four male correspondents and Harriet were in the contingent that made the trip in early October 1916. They traveled under a military escort and remained an entire afternoon. The soldiers were amazed to see Harriet. They had never before seen a woman in one of these trenches. There she was, camera in hand, unafraid, smiling and secure.

As the correspondents made their way through the front-lines, a rain of German shells began to explode while bullets whistled. Harriet took refuge in an underground dugout.

Harriet didn't expect the large variety of comforts the soldiers showed her in their dugouts. She was impressed by what she saw: "Frying pans! Sakes alive: I think I saw every kind of a frying pan that was ever made in the dugouts in the French trenches where men are living like moles and fighting like tigers. . . Many of the 'homes' were complete with well made beds, good cook stoves, musical instruments and even flower beds outside the door and above the top of the trenches."

It was the flowers that most touched Harriet. As she was about to leave, a soldier reached above the trenches and picked her a bouquet of red poppies, white daisies and blue cornflowers. The other correspondents quickly gathered for a picture opportunity. The photo appeared throughout the world press—a young soldier, a brave woman and a bouquet of flowers.

This photo of Harriet, a French solider, and a bouquet of flowers appeared throughout the world press.

It was soon time to return home. Harriet, along with a group of 325 other passengers, left Bordeaux for New York on October 7. She had experienced war and now wanted to tell America about it, to tell the story of the French people's bravery—and to raise money to aid their cause.

They boarded the French liner *Lafayette* when German submarines were torpedoing the American coast. The passengers were so fearful of submarine attacks they spent the majority of their time on deck in life jackets in case of explosion.

When Harriet arrived home, she began touring and speaking on behalf of the war effort. She also planned to write about the Native Americans and to visit every reservation as she lectured about the war. She carried a Corona typewriter with her to write between lectures.

Sometimes she spoke six times in one day, taken from small town to small town by representatives of the Council of Defense in Washington. She retained this pace until the Armistice, usually financing her own expenses. The Council of Defense had little resources. She chose the small towns to speak in because they were ignored by the more famous speakers, and she felt they deserved a chance to hear her words as well as donate to the cause.

People continually asked her if she wasn't afraid to be within the firing line. She would answer, "Why should I when thousands of French women are living in towns which are being constantly bombarded?"

Her tours brought in thousands of dollars for war relief.

Following a talk in Stockton, where she netted $281.75 for the relief fund, she said, "Within three days these Stockton dollars will be feeding the starving children coming down from the devastated region of Rheims, where at the first of the week one of the most terrific battles of the war was waged."

Harriet had traveled to the front as a correspondent—but would forever be remembered as a humanitarian.

RETURN TO SOUTH AMERICA

Harriet's search for the ancestors of America's native population led her on one more quest—to visit every linguistic branch of aboriginal America from Alaska to Tierra del Fuego. As she lectured on behalf of the war effort, she visited every reservation. She also visited historic sites and museums related to that region's Native Americans.

Harriet was convinced an original language had existed during prehistoric times and that as people moved and developed their own cultures language changed and created the present diversity. Nine different groups of North American Indian languages existed. Many overlapped between the United States and Mexico or between Canada, the Northern territories and the United States. She felt this supported her theory about the common origin of many tribes in South and Central America and in southern North America.

Harriet wanted to revisit South America to update her lectures and articles. In 1919 and 1920, her return included frontiers not reached on former journeys. She traversed the entire length of Chile, making a pleasure stop at the Island of

Chiloe. She also studied the Arancanian Indians. From Chile she journeyed to Argentina, Paraguay, Eastern Bolivia, Uruguay and Brazil, where she spent time in Buenos Aires and Rio de Janeiro.

This was not her first return to South America since her and Frank's two-and-a-half-year journey. In the fall of 1909 she made a trip on the Transandine railway, the final link in the 888 miles of rail that connected Buenos Aires on the Atlantic with Valparaiso on the Pacific.

The Transandine railroad consisted of several different companies placing their lines together. This made for an interesting trip as passengers had to change trains often. Once at the summit they sped down steep grades, through tunnels cut out of solid rock, across dizzying bridges. Valparaiso was reached by express train in a few hours. The trip across the continent took slightly over three days (including a mule trip). The return trip through the Summit Tunnel took thirty-four hours—far different from her earlier Andes explorations.

Harriet continued to take trips: to the Amazon; to the historic city of Cajamara where Pizarro met Atahualpa, the last of the Inca rulers; overland down the Chilean Coast to the lake country of South Chile. Her mode of travel varied from train to sailing ship to saddle and canoe. She decided the title "Paris of the New World" now belonged to Buenos Aires, ranking it among the great capitals of the world. Describing "its brilliantly illuminated avenues and dazzling cafes, its beautiful Park of Palermo . . ." she called it gorgeous.

Harriet enjoyed telling stories of her trips to reporters and lecture audiences: "A cafe proprietor in Buenos Aires wished to prepare for the heavy American tourist travel expected in Argentina this year. He consulted with a British resident of the capital with interesting results. A glittering electric sign above his cafe now reads: Fried Potatoes and Champagne." To illustrate her story Harriet showed the incandescent menu on the screen during her lecture.

Of all the articles Harriet wrote over the years, her story on "Rio de Janeiro, in the Land of Lure" in *National Geographic* drew the most attention. Gilbert Grosvenor said, "I regard your Rio story as one of the very best that you have written and I am sure our readers will greatly enjoy it . . ."

The story read in part: "In splendor of hue and setting, this great city of the South is unrivaled the world over. Here granite peak and turquoise sea, tropic forest and rainbow-tinted town, meet and harmonize . . ." The article moved the reader through a spectacular scenic journey to this city perched on several mountains. The Instituto Historico e Geographico Brazileiro honored Harriet in 1920 for the article.

Following the trail of the Conquistadors, she went to the Azores, Madeira, Portugal and Spain, then followed "things Spanish" into Moorish Africa. She and her sister Anna spent a year of travel and research in Spain and Morocco. They criss-crossed French and Spanish Morocco in every imaginable conveyance—mule carts, ox-carts, mountain railways—even an ancient automobile.

All places that had belonged to Spain through the ages dominated Harriet's travel plans. She knew every foot of the

Iberian peninsula, from the rock of Gibraltar at its southern tip, to the tall Pyrean mountains across its northern border. Not content with Madrid and Seville, Barcelona and the parts of Granada all tourists knew, she dug into the remote towns, traveling through the forbidding mountains edging Portugal. Harriet and her sister Anna, in 1923-24, traveled together to French and Spanish Morocco. As usual, they had another unique adventure. On a spring evening their train from Oran in western Algeria chugged into the town of Ujda just over the French-Moroccan border. Harriet felt they had entered a land of romance and mystery by the back door (the new front door being Casablanca).

Originally, they had intended to sail from Oran to Gibraltar and down to Casablanca. The porter at the hotel suggested an automobile from Ujda to Fez, then the railroad to Casablanca, commenting they would see more. They could take only sixty pounds of luggage and shipped the rest by sea to Gibraltar. Spring had arrived in western Algeria as they traveled eight hours by rail from Oran to Ujda. The sisters delighted in the luxuriant green scenes, with wild flowers sprouting everywhere.

From the station in Ujda they went to a small hotel across from the 'jitney' garage. That's when they discovered the automobile service turned out to be a 'jitney line,' one improvised without a great deal of attention paid to comfort. They were the first foreign travelers to apply for passage on it. The line was patronized by Moors and Algerians, Oran Jews and an occasional French commercial traveler. They met no tourists, but many natives during the journey.

At four in the morning, they started on the day's journey in a torrential downpour. The women could not have imagined a more eerie entrance into old Morocco. Shadowy figures passed on the highway in the gray dawn—hooded, shrouded in ghostly white, creeping along with their flocks or prodding their laden donkeys. All of it seemed to belong to an age long past. How happy Harriet was to have listened to the porter's advice.

At the end of these journeys, Harriet said: "I feel now that I have collected information that will take a lifetime to study. I have seen more than one lifetime could hope to fathom. But I have done enough to call attention to some new things. And it is now my life work to formulate the results of my travel. It is these results I am looking to, and not back at the adventures."

FOUNDING A SOCIETY

Harriet accumulated honors over the years. In June 1913 the Royal Geographical Society of London selected Harriet as a member. She was the first American woman to receive the honor, and only the third woman ever to be selected. She was elected a corresponding member of the Geographical Society of Philadelphia in 1911.

Latin America showed its appreciation of her honest appraisal and love of both the area and the people by showering her with several awards and memberships in prestigious groups. She was elected a corresponding member of the Geographic Societies of La Paz, Bolivia; Lima, Peru; and Rio de Janerio, Brazil. The Legion of the Dominican Republic sent her a letter of appreciation, and she became an honorary member of the Academy of Science and Art of Cadiz.

While she appreciated the honors bestowed upon her, Harriet was frustrated that women were always secondary members of most geographic societies. Even she could never be a full member of the National Geographic Society, despite her years of work with the organization and her friendship with Gilbert Grosvenor. Why not have our own group, Harriet wondered?

Harriet joined the discussion on forming a society for women geographers. She was fascinated by the idea and quickly bought a train ticket to New York City where nine women and Harriet met in March 1925. Their goal was to determine what such a group might accomplish.

They finally resolved to form a group with a specific goal. The name selected for the organization was the Society of Woman Geographers. The stated goal was to bring together women explorers whose work involved extensive travel in their investigations of little known or unique places, people, or things. The membership qualifications were the attainment of high achievement in the field. It was decided to include in the society those women distinguished in geographical work whether in allied sciences, ethnology, archaeology, botany, natural history, sociology, folklore or arts and crafts. Only those women who had "done distinctive work (adding) to the world's store of knowledge" were allowed active membership.

Harriet became the first chairperson of the Executive Council in May 1925, and the society's first president in December 1925. She accepted the challenge with her usual vigor and took on, almost single-handedly, the task of nurturing the new society. Within three years membership reached across the United States.

Harriet understood how to structure an organization for success and insisted on having high standards for active

Harriet presents Amelia Earhart the Society of Woman Geographer's first honorary medal.

membership, limiting it to those who, by publishing the results of their studies, added to the world's knowledge of some portion of the globe. She encouraged a corresponding membership composed of those who fulfilled requirements of active membership but lived in foreign countries. She also welcomed as associate members widely traveled women who were interested in aiding geographical exploration and research but had not yet attained a high level of professionalism.

Involvement in the society became so much a part of Harriet's life that she relegated her own career to second place. She spent innumerable hours drafting the hundreds of encouraging letters sent to women in all parts of the world. She also spent a great deal of time contacting women of outstanding geographical attainment, alerting them to the opportunity of membership in the society and encouraging them to join.

The founders saw their vision of the group become reality through Harriet's constant work. "Sparkling enthusiasm" were the words most often used to describe Harriet and what she tried to accomplish as leader of the society. She worked with very little money and no home or office for the organization, often saying the "office was in her heart."

Harriet built a membership that represented forty-three countries. The members had expertise in a wide variety of fields, including archaeology, ethnology, arts and crafts, botany, folklore, mountain climbing, history, sociology, zoology and aviation. Exhausted, she handed the presidency to someone else in June 1933 and was made honorary president.

Society members saluted her: "It was not an easy task, mothering and nurturing this group from a tiny nucleus to a widespread organization, unifying its widely separated members into a whole. But Harriet Adams sent out her own fresh energy and enthusiasm till it vibrated throughout the organization even to its most distant parts, and today the Society of Woman Geographers stands as a monument to her vision, her zeal and her devotion."

In the early 1930s, the society decided to present medals to outstanding women in their field. Amelia Earhart received the first medal on January 5, 1933, in New York City. Harriet, as presenter, said: "I am glad that it is my privilege to present to Miss Earhart, who is one of us, and who has so greatly achieved, the first medal awarded by the Society of Woman Geographers . . . perhaps no others can so fully understand and appreciate as we fellow Geographers of your own sex, whose background and battles have been similar to your own, not only the stupendous courage, but the intelligence and the energy, the grim determination through the years which made possible this crowning achievement of yours."

Those words also expressed Harriet's pride in the Society of Woman Geographers and its place of honor in geographic circles that continues to this day.

FINAL JOURNEY

In 1926 Harriet received the worst news of her life when a Spanish doctor said, "You'll never walk again." She was only fifty-one and had trouble believing her ears. Never to walk again? With all the places still unvisited? Tibet? Baghdad? The Himalayas?

Harriet had suffered an accident an island off of Spain's eastern coast. While exploring the seacoast she slipped in the dark and fell off a cliff. Fishermen found her lying on the rocks, half submerged by the tide. Roping her on a board, they carried her gently to the nearest village. Newspaper reports commented, "The medical care was better in intention than in scientific skill. No one knew how badly she was hurt, no one had an X-ray to find out." That's when the doctor delivered the horrible news. But she refused to accept such a diagnosis, even as she returned by ship to the United States strapped to a rigid board.

Back home the news continued to be bad. Doctors told her the broken bits of vertebrae had shattered in the fall and would never knit. She would be an invalid for the rest of her life. For two years Harriet lay encased in a plaster cast and steel braces, strapped to a board, rigid and uncomplaining, giving her body time to heal itself. Through it all she remained busy as president of the Society of Woman Geographers.

She was determined to conquer her injury, however, and to be able to return to her old way of life. Harriet's persistence paid off. In the winter of 1928 she announced she would walk and added: "I will travel again." She wanted to complete her long projected plan to visit every country touched by Spanish and Moorish civilizations.

In June she left her restricted environment and was ready to set out alone on a seven months' tour of Spain, Africa and Asia Minor. Frank realized travel was the only medicine to make Harriet well. She sailed to the Mediterranean, planning to visit Damascus, Syria, Palestine, Tunis, Algeria, French and Spanish Morocco and Spain. The sea voyage and her return to travel helped her physically and mentally. Before the trip was over she insisted she was "as good as new."

Her travel wasn't limited to boat and train. She caravaned over jarring roads and refused to give into pain. She admitted later that the pain had been incredible at times, but after the trip she felt she had won a victory.

In March 1929, Harriet and Frank set out on another journey to Spain and Portugal. Harriet completed her long-ago projected tour of every country that ever belonged to Spain or Portugal—twenty in all.

In Spain they visited Cadiz, Seville and Barcelona. When they returned to the coast, they separated. Franklin returned to Washington, D.C., and Harriet went on to Spanish Morocco. From there her itinerary included France, Italy, Switzerland, Yugoslavia, Austria, Hungary, Rumania, Turkey, Greece, Syria, Palestine, Transjordania, Egypt, Italian North Africa and Sicily. She wrote: "I completed on this trip firsthand knowledge of every country bordering the Mediterranean. I had never previously been to Rumania, Turkey in Asia, Syria and Libya. Now I have visited every country in the old world or the new, in Europe, Asia, Africa and the islands of the seas that was ever Spain's or Portugal's . . ."

Harriet was fascinated by airplanes and envisioned flying over the territories she had traveled more than twenty-five years before on foot, horseback and by canoe. She was convinced that aviation was destined to mean marvelous things to world explorers. Harriet experienced plane travel for the first time in 1930. She reported, "It's such an experience to fly in a day over some of the places I've taken weeks to travel by land. In the desert to see the land from above is to really understand it. I learned from air trips in Africa, when I saw those dunes stretch so far from north to south, just why my caravan journeys had seemed so roundabout."

During Harriet's 1930 East Africa trip, she attended the coronation of Emperor Haile Selassie I of Ethiopia. This time Harriet journeyed with her sister Anna, who lived in San Francisco. Together they sailed from New York City, visited Spain and France, then sailed for Port Said in Egypt. At that point their paths separated; Anna to Palestine and Harriet to Ethiopia. They planned to meet a month later in Cairo.

On her way to the coronation, Harriet visited several towns along the Red Sea and in French Somaliland. After the coronation she would continue travel in Eastern Africa and up the Persian Gulf.

Her coronation trip caused a sensation in the press: "Within the week this adventurous spirit is setting forth again upon her travels. Attendance at the coronation of the Emperor of Ethiopia is the most picturesque event in her itinerary . . . and it is quite possible that she may be the recipient of the formal gift of honor, which for a woman is a white mule."

The press was enchanted by Harriet's wardrobe. "A wardrobe ranging from flying suits to evening dresses and adapted to both summer and winter climates of fourteen countries is necessary for Mrs. Harriet Chalmers Adams . . . on her latest journey."

While Harriet was not an official delegate to the coronation, she received great publicity because of her fame. During and after the ceremony, she stayed with the United States Minister to Abyssiania and his wife.

Then bad news arrived. Anna had become ill in Palestine. Harriet hurriedly joined her but Anna died days after her arrival. Harriet somberly accompanied Anna's ashes to San Francisco for burial

Frank retired on January 1, 1934, after working at the Pan-American Union for twenty-five years. The Adamses decided to live on the Mediterranean, basing themselves in Spain. From there they would travel. Their possessions were placed in storage. Years of photographs, motion pictures and research facts were boxed, waiting for Harriet to compile the material into books. Unfortunately, the storage of the materials was tragic. A leaking water pipe soaked the notes and photographs beyond repair. Today, all that remains of Harriet's life work are the pictures and articles she published during her life, plus her six scrapbooks of newspaper clippings and memorabilia.

Harriet sailed first, traveling in the late summer of 1933 to Palestine. She told reporters she hoped to find a quiet spot to write articles about her travels. Frank would join her in early winter. The time spent in Palestine was typical of previous trips—seeing the unknown, spending time with the people.

After leaving the Mideast, she traveled to England via Italy and Algeria and joined Frank at South Hampton. Then they were off to the island of Madiera, Spain, where they spent the winter.

Their life settled into a hectic pattern. Winters were spent in Spain, or Yugoslavia or Athens after Frank became fascinated with the Balkans. Summers meant travel throughout Europe and Asia Minor. Their pace was so hurried that even Harriet wrote at one point "after a year of wandering, we are glad to feel settled for a time."

Harriet wanted to settle and focus on writing. But travel, talking with people and research still took the majority of her time. She continued to write travel articles for *National Geographic* and other magazines, but did not find time to begin her book. Instead, she wrote a series of newsletters once a week for twenty-six weeks. Each of them was from a different city. These were recorded and broadcast throughout the United States.

Harriet grew homesick and longed to return to the United States. But Frank wanted to continue traveling and thought it would be too expensive to live in America. Harriet consented, saying in a letter to a friend, "Nothing for me to do but make the best of it and his happiness comes first with me as it always has. We are so rich in having one another."

"Why all this travel?" they were once asked.

Harriet answered, "Both my husband and I have traveled, first of all, for the mere love of going."

But the couple's traveling schedule was slowed when Harriet's health began to fail. In November 1936, she became seriously ill with a kidney inflammation. The Adamses spent the winter of 1936-37 relaxing in Athens, and Harriet felt she had recovered.

The next spring found them in Nice, relaxing in southern France and enjoying the culture. Frank had hoped Harriet's illness would subside, and that the warm air, friends, and a congenial atmosphere would help Harriet recover her health. But this was not the case.

Harriet died in Nice on July 17, 1937. She was 62.

Harriet's hometown paper, *The Stockton Evening Record*, wrote in their obituary: "Harriet Chalmers Adams' contribution to man's knowledge of his own sphere will remain although she has embarked on the greatest journey of all."

Harriet's death was announced in dozens of newspapers and magazines, including *Time*, the *London Times,* and newspapers throughout South America where she was loved and respected.

Before her death Harriet had become a citizen of the world, recognized not only as an explorer, writer and lecturer but as a humanitarian and promoter of better relations between nations. Her concern for native people throughout the world was well-known and mentioned in every tribute. The accounts also emphasized her exploration, writing and lecturing and the fact she was the wife of Franklin Pierce Adams. While they had been separated many times, the last four years had been spent together. Frank's grief was devastating. His correspondence reflected his sadness. " . . something I come across of Harriet's just gives me such heart pangs and mental disturbance. Everything about me in all the memories of her are so fragrant with her sweet spirit. . .These are sad days for me— the first anniversary . . . Harriet's personality was so potent that I feel her presence and guidance. Her little voice has corrected me so many years that I can hear—'Don't do that Frank dear'—so often and I check myself and do the way she wished. . . I've made some progress toward adjustment—but it is naturally slow indeed. We had such a gloriously happy life together—the void so vast." Frank died three years after Harriet.

The Society of Women Geographers passed a resolution in December 1937 entitled *In Remembrance of Harriet Chalmers Adams.* Sisters from the society, fellow writers and photographers, geographers and friends also wrote tributes for a special February 1938 publication dedicated to Harriet's memory.

While the tributes acknowledged Harriet's travels and explorations, her interest in people commanded the most attention: "She was more genuinely interested in other people's problems and ambitions than anyone I ever knew," wrote Blair Niles, one of the founders of the Society of Women Geographers.

"Lovely to look upon and with a natural charm and sympathy that radiated from her intelligent and understanding personality, HCA possessed the rare quality of achieving her difficult objective, together with the gift of making friends and establishing confidence in her work among peoples in every walk of life, whether rulers of enlightened nations or simple natives in primitive jungles," wrote John Oliver LaGroce, vice president of the National Geographic Society.

As a final tribute, the Society of Women Geographers established a *Harriet Chalmers Adams Memorial Endowment Fund*.

The little girl from Stockton, California, had lived the life of adventure she sought and had gained the love, respect and admiration of millions the world over in the process.

BIBLIOGRAPHY

Adams, Franklin Pierce, *Papers*. Library of Congress.

_____, *Personnel File*, Bureau of American Republics.

Adams, Harriet Chalmers. *Personal Scrapbooks*. Stockton-San Joaquin County Public Library, Stockton, California.

_____. *Personal Journals* (In private hands)

_____. *Papers*. Library of Congress.

_____. *Correspondence with Gilbert Grosvenor, President, National Geographic Society*. Archives, National Geographic Society, Washington, D. C.

Crosby, Susan. *Harriet Chalmers Adams*. Thesis, San Joaquin Delta College, Stockton, California, May 1983.

Davis, M. Kathryn. *The Forgotten Life of Harriet Chalmers Adams: Geographer, Explorer, Feminist.* Master s Thesis, California State University, San Francisco, April 1995.

"Harriet Chalmers Adams, Our Fabulous Foremother." *California History Magazine*, March 1, 1987, 32-3.

James, Edward T., Editor. *Notable American Women, 1607-1950.*

Martin, V. Covert. *Stockton Album: Through the Years.* Stockton, CA: Siard Printing Company, 1959.

Who Was Who in America, Volume 1, 1897-1942. Chicago: The A.N.Marquis Company, 1942.

Works by Harriet Chalmers Adams

Adams, Harriet Chalmers. "Picturesque Paramaribo: The City Which Was Exchanged for New York." *The National Geographic Magazine,* June 1907.

_____. "East Indians in the New World." *The National Geographic Magazine,* July 1907.

_____. "Along the Old Inca Highway." *The National Geographic Magazine,* April 1908.

_____. "Some Wonderful Sights in the Andean Highlands." *The National Geographic Magazine,* September 1908.

_____. "Cuzco, America's Ancient Mecca." *The National Geographic Magazine,* October 1908.

_____. "Kaleidoscopic La Paz: The City of the Clouds." *The National Geographic Magazine,* February 1909.

_____. "The First Transandine Railroad from Buenos Aires to Valparaiso." *The National Geographic Magazine,* May 1910.

_____. "In French Lorraine: That Part of France Where the First American Soldiers Have Fallen." *The National Geographic Magazine,* November-December 1917.

_____. "Rio de Janeiro, In the Land of Lure." *The National Geographic Magazine,* September 1920.

_____. "The Grand Canyon Bridge." The National Geographic Magazine, June 1921.

———. "Volcano-Girded Salvador: A Prosperous Central American State with the Densest Rural Population in the Western World." *The National Geographic Magazine*, February 1922.

———. "A Longitudinal Journey through Chile." *The National Geographic Magazine*, September 1922.

———. "Adventurous Sons of Cadiz." *The National Geographic Magazine*, August 1924.

———. "Across French and Spanish Morocco." *The National Geographic Magazine*, March 1925.

———. "An Altitudinal Journey through Portugal." *The National Geographic Magazine*, November 1927.

———. "Barcelona, Pride of the Catalans." *The National Geographic Magazine*, March 1929.

———. "Cirenaca, Eastern Wing of Italian Libya." *The National Geographic Magazine*, June 1930.

———. "Madrid Out-of-Doors." *The National Geographic Magazine*, August 1931.

———. "River-Encircled Paraguay." *The National Geographic Magazine*, April 1933.

———. "Madeira The Fluorescent." *The National Geographic Magazine*, July 1934.

———. "European Outpost: The Azores." *The National Geographic Magazine*, January 1935.

———. "Go Home and Look for Work." *Harpers Weekly*, August 29, 1914.

———. "Star-Spangled Banner Guardians." *World Outlook*, February 1915.

_____. "Uncle Sam's White Magic." *World Outlook*, April 1915.

_____. "Espana Pacifica y Prospera." T*he World's Work Magazine*, October 1915.

_____. "Side-lights on Latin American Trade." *World Outlook*, November 1915.

_____. "Women of Other Americas." *Ladies Home Journal*, October 1916.

_____. "The Truth About Spain and Primo de Rivera." *TheAmerican Review of Reviews*, January 1925.

Adams, Harriet Chalmers and Franklin P. Adams. "The Liberation of Bolivia." *The American Review of Reviews*, January 1913.

INDEX

Academy of Art of Cadiz, 93
Adams, Frank, 14, 16-20, 22-24, 30-32, 34-36, 38, 39, 41-42, 45-46, 48-58, 63-64, 70, 72-73, 76, 99, 102-104
Adams, Harriet (Chalmers)
  Amelia Earhart and, 95, 97
  birth, 9
  childhood, 9-14
  marriage, 16
  death, 103
  education, 13
  founds the Society of Woman Geographers, 94-97
  injury, 98-99
  obituararies, 103-105
  photographer, 18-19
  physical appearance, 14, 16
  receives honors , 93
  recovery from jury, 99
  travels in: Algeria, 91, 102; Argentina, 48, 49-51, 89, 90; Azores, 90; Asia, 69-71, 76-78; Austria, 100; Bolivia, 22, 24, 26, 49, 51; Brazil, 51-52; Chile, 48; Colombia, 55; Cuba, 64; Curacao, 54; Ecuador, 20; England, 102; Egypt, 100; El Salvador, 19; Ethiopia, 100-101; France, 80-86, 99-100, 103; French Guiana, 52, 54; Greece, 100, 102-103; Haiti, 63-68; Italy, 100, 102; Mexico, 16-17; Morocco, 90-92, 99; Palestine, 100-102; Panama, 20, 55; Paraquay, 51, 53; Peru, 20-22, 27-32, 34-48; Portugal, 90, 99; Rumania, 100; Sicily, 100; Syria, 100; Spain, 90-91, 98-102; Switzerland, 100; Yugoslavia, 100, 102
  travels with father, 9-14
  war correspondent, 79-87
  war relief effort, 86-87
  writer/lecturer, 56-62
Adams, Henry, 14,
American Fund for French Wounded, 80

"Andean Wonderland, The", 62,
Arancanian, 89
Associated Advertising Clubs of America, 60
Atahualpa, 89
Aymara, 26, 49, 76
Aztec, 17, 78

Big Geography, The, 38,
Bulletin, The, 79

Chalmers, Alexander, 9-13, 19
Chalmers, Anna, 90-91, 100-101
Chunchos, 39
Chalmers, Fannie, 10, 19,
Chalmers, George, 10
Columbus, Bartholomew, 66
Columbus, Christopher, 63-64, 66, 68
Council of Defense, 86

Earhart, Amelia, 95, 97

Geographical Society of Philadelphia, 93
Grosvenor, Gilbert, 57, 90

Haile Selassie I, Emperor, 100
Harpers Magazine, 80

Ifugao, 76,
In Remembrance of Harriet Chalmers Adams, 104
Inca, 78
Inca Mining and Rubber Company, The, 26
Instituto Historico e Geographico Brazilerio, 90

La Groce, John Oliver, 105
Lafayette, The, 86
Legion of the Dominican Republic, 93
London Times, The, 104
Lusitania, 79

Mayan, 17, 78
Moros, 73,

National Geographic Magazine, The, 57-58, 80, 90, 102
National Geographic Society, The, 57-58, 76, 105
Niles, Blair, 105

Old Inca Highway, 42

Pan America Commercial Conference, 58-60,
Pan American Union (Bureau of American Republics), 17, 56, 58
Panama Canal, 20,

Quichua, 31, 44,

"Rio de Janerio, in the Land of Lure", 90
Royal Geographical Society, 93

Society of Women Geographers, 94-97, 99, 104-105
Solenodons, 63-65,
soroche, 26,
Stockton Evening Record, 103
Stockton Gas and Electric Company, 14

Taft, William Howard, 60,
Time, 104
Toltec, 78

Vassar Brothers' Institute, 62
Vassar Lecture Series, 58

Washington Post, The, 69

Zuni-Hopi, 78,